W. E. (William Edward) Hickson

Tracts for Inquirers

No. II Reform illusions

W. E. (William Edward) Hickson

Tracts for Inquirers
No. II Reform illusions

ISBN/EAN: 9783337060114

Printed in Europe, USA, Canada, Australia, Japan

Cover: Foto ©ninafisch / pixelio.de

More available books at **www.hansebooks.com**

TRACTS FOR INQUIRERS.

BY

𝕾. 𝕰. 𝕳ickson.

No. II. REFORM ILLUSIONS.

1832.   1867.

2 *Will. IV. c.* 45.   30 *& 31 Vict. c.* 102.

LONDON:

GROOMBRIDGE & SONS, 5 PATERNOSTER ROW.

Price Sixpence.

1867.

PRINTED BY WILLIAMS & STRAHAN, 7 LAWRENCE LANE, CHEAPSIDE, E.C.

ADVERTISEMENT OF THE WORK.

UNDER the title of "*Tracts for Inquirers*," I am proposing to publish a selection from the notes I have been in the habit of making, through many years, on a variety of subjects,—Social, Administrative, Scientific, Musical, and Historical; accompanying them with occasional observations on passing events.

They will be printed in numbers, as a Serial; with an uniform type, and consecutive paging, to admit of ultimate binding; but I do not pledge myself to their issue at fixed intervals. In the present state of my health, and as now in the evening of life, I must present myself to the public, not as an editor bound to say something on a given day, but as one intending to speak only when he has something to say which, although he knows it will not always please, he thinks should be said before his final leave-taking.

As such unavoidable irregularity might lead to a heavier expense for advertising than the undertaking would afford, I must, to avoid it, ask the permission of many to make the work known to them, through the post, by presentation copies; and I shall be glad to be favoured by letter with the names and addresses of those who may either be willing to receive a circular notice of the appearance of a new number, or permit me to place them, for any limited period, on a private list of subscribers.

The price of each I shall endeavour to limit to Sixpence; and, if the case should occur, I shall be happy to meet the views of liberal friends, of ampler means than my own, who may desire reprints of any paper, at a cheaper rate for distribution.

W. E. HICKSON.

Fairseat, Wrotham.
  Kent.

II.

REFORM ILLUSIONS.

1832.   1867.

2 *Will.* IV., *cap.* 45.   30 & 31 *Vict. cap.* 102.

LET me be understood.—Reform is not an illusion ; but it will not be denied, after recent discussions, there may be many illusions about Reform. In reference to which, and to their proper application, the present is a favourable opportunity for a retrospect.

Reform means " amendment," which we all need ; and as applied generally to the removal of the defects of our social institutions, and of those especially which most interfere with the physical and moral welfare of the masses, " Reform " embraces the worthiest objects of human ambition. But every man who sees the necessity of changes, consequent upon altered states of a population, is not equally a judge of the changes required. It is possible to suppose ourselves correcting abuses, when we are only extending them ; and on the part of statesmen, philosophers, and philanthropists, in all ages, this has been, and remains, one of the commonest illusions of mankind.

B

From the days of Lycurgus to our own, how many schemes of
social regeneration have not been set on foot; how many experiments
in the science of government have not been tried? Republics of
every conceivable pattern ; oligarchical, democratical, hierarchal ;
military despotisms, limited monarchies, church and state alliances ;
—one after another rising, flourishing, fading, and disappearing !
The results in each case widely different, but all generally disappoint-
ing. Their history a record of mistakes ; supplying a self-seeking
class of politicians, with an apology for indolence, and their own
personal participation in abuses seen to be profitable, and conse-
quently therefore assumed to be inevitable ; and leaving even on
better minds, an impression somewhat discouraging to patriotic
effort ; as when Pope wrote :—

> " For forms of government let fools contest ;
> That which is best administered is best."

I notice these often quoted lines as embodying, with a profound
truth, a verbal fallacy ; for if there be any where a best, or one system
of administration better than another, there must have been causes
for it ; and the nature of those causes, and the precise difference
between one system of administration and another, there can be no
folly in discussing. Pope, we may be sure, did not deny this. He
meant only to rebuke the partisanship, which overlooks the object
for which governments exist. Constitutions are of no value, but as
means to an end. The prosperity of states is dependent solely upon
the intelligence by which they are guided ; whether as displayed in
the councils of Kings, or of Presidents. The form of administration concerns the happiness of a people only so far as it may lead
to good, or bad measures of administration ; and, as we cannot have
wise measures of administration without wise heads to frame them,
the practical question for all of us, in times of revolutionary or reform
excitement, is simply, whether the changes brought about or proposed by popular leaders, are of a kind to give the direction of affairs
to our worthiest and ablest citizens, or to the most mercenary and
incapable.

This is the question, which if we ask now, we need not wait for the answer soon to be given by events. We may anticipate it from the teachings of the past.

An old diary brings vividly before me the culminating incidents of the last serious Reform agitation : a generation back.

1830.

June 26.—Death of George IV.

July 31.—Revolution in France. After three days' fighting in Paris, Charles X. deposed.

Aug. 5.—General election in England. Henry Brougham returned for the county of York.

,,   9.—Louis Philippe, Duke of Orleans, after assenting to certain amendments of the Charter of Louis XVIII., elected, by the Chamber of Deputies, King of the French.

,,   25.—Revolution in Brussels ; resulting in the separation of Belgium from Holland ;—joined together by the allied powers in 1815 as the Kingdom of the Netherlands.

Sep. 15.—Opening of the Manchester and Liverpool railroad : the first in England for the conveyance of passengers. The opening marred by a fatal accident to Mr. Huskisson, our Free Trade minister.*

Nov. 2.—Notices of motion by Earl Grey and Henry Brougham, for Reform, met by the Prime Minister,—the Duke of Wellington, with the declaration, that "the legislature could not be improved," and that "the people would be quiet if let alone."

,,   9.—Threatened riot in the City. Abandonment in consequence of the proposed visit of William IV.—to dine with the Lord Mayor.

,,   15.—Majority of 29 against the Cabinet of the Duke of Wellington, on a question of the Civil List. Followed by resignation of Ministers.

,,   22.—Earl Grey, First Lord of the Treasury. Henry Brougham raised to the Peerage, with the title of Lord Brougham and Vaux, and made Lord Chancellor.

,,   29.—Insurrection in Poland, crowned with temporary success.

---

* A cloud upon an otherwise bright day in my personal history—that of my marriage.

Feb 3.—Announcement by Viscount Althorp, that the Cabinet which he represented as Chancellor of the Exchequer, had prepared a Reform Bill.

Great was the interest this announcement occasioned, and public expectation was wrought up to the highest possible pitch of excitement when, on the 1st of March, the Bill alluded to was introduced in the House of Commons by Lord John Russell. I call to mind its effect on a circle of friends, with whom I was passing the evening of that day. One of them, (William Lawrence, the late Alderman, and father of the present Member,) stood up and read the first published particulars of the measure, from an early copy of the *Globe*:— "Sixty rotten boroughs to be disfranchised; forty-seven small boroughs to return each one member instead of two; representatives to be given to all the large towns. In boroughs, all rated householders of £10 per annum to be entitled to vote; in counties all leaseholders of £50, &c." The measure was so much more liberal than the reader had anticipated, that it seemed to take away his breath. As he concluded, another of our company,—the late Rev. Robert Aspland, rose from his seat, and striking a table near him with the palm of his hand, said solemnly " thank God !"

How we shook hands and congratulated one other in those days! the ministerial scheme uniting all sections of Reformers; Hume speaking of it as a measure " far surpassing his most sanguine hopes," and Macaulay describing it as " a great, a glorious, and a comprehensive plan;" and how we determined to rally round " the Bill, the whole Bill, and nothing but the Bill;" for, as the Bill would unseat, and send in search of new constituencies, no less than 168 members, a fierce opposition was to be expected. This was soon shewn. On the 22nd March the second reading was carried by a majority of only 1,—(302 against 301); and this majority was converted, in Committee, on the night of Thursday, the 20th of April, into a minority of 22. Upon which, the very next day, William IV. went down in person to Westminster, and prorogued the House;— " to give my people an opportunity of expressing their sense of a great question."

Ministers had tendered their resignation, with the alternative of an appeal to the country; and the King, having decided upon supporting them, had acted upon his resolve with a promptitude which took the House by surprise, and produced a demonstration of popular enthusiasm rarely witnessed. New writs were issued on the Saturday, and the following Monday, Tuesday, and Wednesday were days of a spontaneous general illumination. On Wednesday, indeed, not only was the metropolis a blaze of light, but it was remarked that from the Land's End to John O'Groat's, there was scarcely an obscure hamlet in which lamps* or candles were not exhibited. For had the dissolution not made it certain that now, by an effort, the Reform Bill would be safe ? And did not Reform mean the putting an end to all wrong doing, and the return from Heaven of Astrea, Goddess of Justice, to restore the Golden Age ?

We are still waiting for Astrea, but the result of the new elections was as triumphant as could have been desired by those who expected it to secure her advent. The new House of Commons, after the re-introduction of the Reform Bill, gave a majority for its second reading (June 24th) of 136. Further difficulties were confined to the resistance of a not very large majority of the Peers, and would not have been serious, had not that resistance led to further outdoor demonstrations, which, in the angry state of the public mind, could no longer be restrained within peaceful limits ; and which demonstrations, alarming timid friends of the Monarchy, produced a vacillating policy on the part of the Court. On the rejection of the Bill by the Lords (October 7th, 1831),† riots sprang up at Derby, Nottingham, and Bristol, on a scale which reminded many then living of the Lord George Gordon Riots in June, 1780, when thirty-six houses, set on fire by the mob, were counted blazing at one time. Bristol

---

* My Journal notices, incidentally, the price of illumination lamps rising suddenly to 12s. per dozen, and a neighbour spending upon them, and the oil they required, £80 for his share of the national rejoicing.

† After a five nights' debate, when 199 Peers divided against 158. Majority, (which included 20 of the Bishops.) 41.

was in the power of a similar mob for the two whole days and nights of October 29th and 30th, 1831; during which the prisons of the town were broken open with sledge hammers, debtors and criminals released, spirit shops were attacked for drink, and the houses of obnoxious individuals plundered and burnt. In those two days property to the amount of £500,000 was destroyed; and 110 persons were killed and wounded, or otherwise injured. The immediate provocation of this riot was only the entry into the town of an unpopular recorder (Sir Charles Wetherell); and the unfavourable impression it made on the minds of the governing classes was not improved by the news which arrived, three weeks later, that the Trades unions of Lyons had risen in arms (November 21st) to establish a tariff of wages, and after many sanguinary conflicts with the military and national guard, in which between 500 and 600 persons were killed, had made themselves masters of the city. An army of 26,000 men, commanded by Marshal Soult, was required to put down this insurrection: the first distinct class insurrection for rights of labour; repeated, (as noticed in my last, p. 11), seventeen years later, in Paris.

These disorders, which had arisen naturally out of the then recent revolution of 1830, (for it is the necessary drawback to all advantages gained by physical force that those who have succeeded by it for one object, will apply it to another,) had some effect in shaking the faith of English Reformers in the doctrine, recently revived, which was, then, very prevalent, that a little frightening of the Aristocracy does no harm; and projects for an armed organisation, corresponding to that of a National Guard, in which Birmingham and Manchester had taken the lead, were for a time laid aside. When, however, in May the Reform Bill was again defeated by the Lords, and Ministers had, in consequence, resigned, popular impatience to try the effect of a rough and violent remedy was again manifested, and helped undoubtedly to render impossible the formation of a new Conservative Cabinet; which, during an interregnum of nine days, Lord Lyndhurst and the Duke of Wellington sought in vain to effect. The Duke then advised the King to restore the Grey Cabinet, withdrawing at the same time his own opposition in the Lords; and the crisis was at an end. The Reform Bill passed its third reading in the Lords June 4th, 1832:—two days before the death, in his 85th year, of Jeremy Bentham; who just lived to be congratulated on the event.

Congratulated! But is that the right word? Do we now pay compliments to each other on the satisfactory state of the National Representation as we then established it? Have we lately heard of Birmingham and Manchester "marching upon London" to support the principles of the Reform Act, or of their coming up by railroad to denounce them?

To denounce them, certainly, as illusory; and illusory they must have been to some extent, inasmuch as the last thing any of us, on the Liberal side, looked for was to see the Tories climb again into power by the very scaffolding we were erecting for ourselves; and to witness a long succession of Parliaments, each of them, with one exception, containing fewer reform elements than the last of the unreformed Parliaments, which we were then superseding.

The one exception was the First Reformed Parliament, elected in December, 1832, when 509 supporters of the Grey cabinet were returned, and only 149 of the opposition; a result, shown afterwards to have been the effect only of panic among the Conservatives, who, supposing themselves utterly beaten, had mostly retired from the field; for the election of January, 1835, under the auspices of Sir Robert Peel, when the panic had subsided, and Registration Societies had mastered the position, reduced the total of the Whig and Radical ranks from 509 to 316. A majority of 10, only, was all that Lord John Russell obtained in his second Parliament, on the first division taken as a trial of strength,—that of February 9th, 1835,—for the choice of Speaker! One hundred reformers had lost their seats;—seats destined, from that time to the present, not to be fully recovered.

I call attention to the very striking fact, that excepting the short

interval of twenty-three months in 1833-4, no such Liberal majorities have been seen in the House of Commons as those which were
obtained in the last of the unreformed Parliaments.—A majority for
the Reform Bill, as before observed, of 136, (June 24th, 1831), and
of 162, on its third introduction ; the second reading being in the
last instance carried (December 12th) by 324 against 162,—or
exactly two to one.

These majorities were the result of an appeal to an electoral body
believed to have been under 200,000, for the whole of the United
Kingdom !

The author of the *Black Book* was then reminding us (p. 601)
that the number of electors in England who actually voted at the
election of 1830 was estimated at only 87,000, and cheering us at the
same time with the assurance (p. 607) that " the Reform Bill would
substitute for this oligarchy with selfish and limited interests, a national
government responsible to 500,000 electors, every one of whom has
an interest in domestic peace, order, and prosperity." Instead of
500,000, the several Reform Acts produced a registered body of
electors for Great Britain and Ireland, in 1832, of 812,935. The
extension was, therefore, considerable; and as in 1866 the number of
registered electors had, from the growth of population, further
increased to somewhat above 1,350,000, it would surely have
been wise to have asked ourselves, before repeating the same kind of
experiment, why this large addition of voters so completely failed
of ensuring the ends of a true representation that, for thirty years,
we have seen the government of this country not in the hands of a
fair majority of any shade of opinion, but dependent upon a new
oligarchy, composed of small and insignificant sections ; which, in the
balancing of parties, by shifting sides at an election, or in the House,
has been able to make and unmake hybrid ministries, and play a
political game of see-saw with the national interests.

This is my short reply to comments received on my last paper,
sent me by honest men, more hopeful of progress, in the true and
proper sense of the word, than I can feel, under the prodigious mis-

takes we are now committing. A correspondent, to whom I bow with respect from his rising reputation at the bar, reminds me of many Liberal objects to which I used to be favourable (and am favourable still), which he thinks would be promoted by almost any kind of reform, which gave a larger basis to the suffrage, although, in other respects, not perfectly satisfactory. He says, " It is useless to dwell upon the deficiencies of the working classes in point of education. They have, at all events, sense enough to discover the men who sincerely desire to raise and improve the masses; and such are the men whom they will elect to Parliament; because popular sympathies are even more important than education for forming sound political opinions."

So, my learned friend, many of us, your senior counsel for Reform, reasoned in 1832 ; and reasoned wrong. Popular sympathies, on their first serious test, were nowhere so infallible as we hoped to find them, in distinguishing the earnest from the plausible ; and often failed us altogether ; declaring not unfrequently against our best men, and showing that the labours of our ablest working administrators had met with slight appreciation from the class they were most to benefit.

I take from the electoral returns of the period another broad fact, which should be included in my friend's brief when next instructed in this case. At the election of May, 1831, to the last unreformed Parliament, *when freeholders alone voted*, the whole of the eighty-two County members returned for England were pledged to Reform, with the exception of six. At the next election, the first under the Reform Act, when the number of County members had been raised to 144, and when £50 tenants at will had been made electors, the proportion of Reformers to Conservatives was at once diminished ; standing as 102 against 42 ; and at the election of January, 1835, these numbers were nearly reversed ; giving a decided majority to the old Tory party, which as far as the Counties are concerned, it has ever since maintained.

This result was partly to be attributed to the introduction of a clause in the Reform Bill, on the motion of the Marquis of Chandos, to include, as County voters, £50 tenants at will, with £50 leaseholders. It was resisted by Lord John Russell, on the ground that while a lease represented some kind of ownership, more than equivalent in many cases to a 40s. freehold, a yearly tenancy was not a possession, and therefore not a corresponding guarantee for electoral indepen- dence ; but the clause was carried against him, through the desertion of Hume, Hodges, Gisborne, and many other Liberals, who voted with the Marquis.* It was a grievous error, and they paid for it. Most unmistakably, the popular sympathies of the agricultural mind were not Radical.

The case of the Boroughs was not precisely similar ; for the Reform Act of 1832, while extending the suffrage, did not lower it. On the contrary, it proceeded some steps in the opposite direction ; abolish- ing the right of making burgesses by gift and purchase, which had been largely abused for election purposes, and disfranchising generally, non-resident freemen ; a large proportion of whom belonged to the poorer class. With a tenderness, however, for vested interests quite at variance with this proceeding, the Act allowed the old fagot voters to retain their privileges, as resident freemen, for themselves, their children and apprentices ; an incon- sistency and weakness of which, it was very early seen, the effect would be deplorable.

At the contest for Liverpool in 1835, when its constituency had been doubled, (8,167 voting instead of the 4,401 in 1830,) the most open bribery prevailed ; during the last hour of the election the price of a vote rose from £15 to £25, and, profiting as well by a division in the Reform ranks, the freemen succeeded in placing a Tory (Lord Sandon) at the head of the poll.

Three years had not then elapsed since we had read in the *Black*

---

* 18th August 1831—

For the Amendment of the Marquis of Chandos 232

Against 148

Majority , ... 84

Book, that the Reform Bill, once passed, " would put an end to the perjuries, drunkenness, riots and immoralities of parliamentary elections !" (p. 607.)

A very little further experience showed us that among our £10 householders, admitted to vote with no other test of qualification than the payment for a twelvemonth of a local rate, there was far too large a proportion as unfitted for an honest and intelligent exercise of the suffrage as pauper freemen; and that in the hap-hazard system we had retained for electoral divisions, (as if the size and distribution of constituencies had been of secondary moment,) there were other elements of danger, all of which together were likely to expose us to the most corrupt influences of the old system ; and even to increase them.

We have had now placed in our hands the Report of the Commissioners appointed to inquire into recent corrupt practices at elections in Great Yarmouth, Lancaster, Reigate, and Totnes ; and turning over their four volumes of evidence, I tax my memory in vain for anything more glaring and abominably vicious in the past than belongs to the present. I recall, before the old Reform Act, many electoral abuses, and a generally defective representation, some instances of which had become a world scandal, but not a state of things in which the seeds of electoral demoralisation had been sown so broadcast over the country as we have seen them under the provisions of the colourable remedy we applied in 1832. The principle of the old Nomination Boroughs was utterly indefensible ; but it yet had its favourable side, as compared with that of bribe-able ignorance, which we, too largely, accepted in exchange. The Commissioners tell us of two-hundred public-houses opened in Great Yarmouth, at the election of 1865, and £6,000 brought down by one candidate in oyster barrels, and £4,000 by another, to debauch the constituents ; but no man was made the worse by an election for Gatton or Old Sarum, and the members returned for such places were at least upon a par for honesty with any of our modern oyster-barrel candidates ; and often men of much higher ability. The oyster-barrel candidate being usually the self-constituted judge of his own fitness, while the member for a Nomination Borough had at least the confidence of a large party, and was often selected by that party less on the ground of family connexions than the usefulness of talent.

The Earl of Chatham, who declared himself in favour of a Reform of the County Representation in 1770, sat originally for Old Sarum: brought in, as plain William Pitt, in 1735, when quite a young man, with only a hundred a year for patrimony, but a high college reputation, to oppose the Tory minister, Sir Robert Walpole. The younger brother of the next Earl, the second William Pitt (who was also a person of narrow means), was, when denouncing, in 1781, the American war, as a war against men "struggling in the holy cause of liberty," and supporting Parliamentary Reform, with the help of Charles James Fox, sitting for Appleby, another of the Nomination Boroughs included among the sixty (reduced finally to fifty-six) disfranchised by Schedule A. The celebrated John Horne Tooke sat for Old Sarum in 1801. "Brougham," observes Mr. H. B. Stanton, " entered the Commons through the narrow door of a Nomination Borough, though he left it with the plaudits of the largest constituency in the kingdom. Burke, Romilly, Mackintosh, and other illustrious and liberal names, were indebted to close corporations for their introduction to senatorial fame."* In more open constituencies we had such men as Byng and Sir Francis Burdett returned for Middlesex in 1802; and looking further back, we see that our old Parliaments, from the days of Hampden, whatever were the anomalies of the representation, never wanted for a good sprinkling of popular leaders, and always contained men of high intellectual reputation, in advance of their time.

Let it be borne in mind, also, that in the days of Charles James Fox, before the timid had become frightened by the too-sweeping violence of the first French Revolution, neither of the two Houses could be described as altogether unfriendly to democratic extension. Mr. Pitt's motion for Reform in 1782 was lost only by 20,

* *Sketches of Reform and Reformers,* p. 166.

in a House of 802 Members. The American Declaration of Independence, July 4th, 1776, was then recent, and its principles had become the political creed of chivalrous members of the French nobility, who had shared in the preceding struggle, and of many Englishmen of rank and fortune. The founders of *The Society for Constitutional Information*, to support the object of Pitt's motion, were Earl Grey and Major Cartwright; while, the same year, (1782,) the Duke of Richmond was taking the lead in forming another association, called " The Quintuple Alliance, for the promotion of Annual Parliaments and Universal Suffrage."

Can we now fairly state that we have in the two Houses a larger body of qualified legislators, genuine friends of the people, than at that epoch ? I think not. No, my friend; it is a mortifying confession, but it is an honest one, the addition of more than a million of voters to our old constituency by the first Reform Act, did not, from the blundering method of that extension, permanently raise the character of the House of Commons. We did not gather grapes of thorns, nor figs of thistles. We did not diminish the general average of the expense of elections, but we largely increased it. We did not shut out from the House place-hunters, private jobbers, and mere party men, but, in a new form, gave them freer entrance than before. We did not secure for legislators a larger number of earnest and thoughtful students of administrative questions, but a smaller number; replacing, sometimes, the few we had, by men as impatient of discussion on " a mere principle," as the most indolent of schoolboys of their first elementary lessons. Men who, instead of proving careful guardians of the public purse, have shown themselves as favourable to lavish expenditure as any of their predecessors; who have left untouched all the old abuses of Army and Navy patronage, and more than doubled, in times of peace, the expenses of our Military and Naval establishments(—£11,657,487 in 1835, £26,179,000 in 1867.*)—Who, within the same period, have raised the general burden of taxation from £45,000,000 to £70,000,000;—

* See Addenda.

mitigated only in its effects by the general increase of wealth, and an addition of six millions to the population. Who, instead of improving our Local government to the extent hoped for, have added to its cost, and impaired its efficiency;—creating new Boards where old Boards should have been consolidated; marring, from the very first, the measures of Municipal and Poor Law Reform, as originally conceived by their authors; throwing upon the Poor rates objects largely "unconnected with relief," until the gross amount is again beginning to swallow up rentals (£9,448,319 in 1864, against £6,973,000 in 1854) ;* and who have to this hour, and chiefly from the poorest of motives, a weakness for " City hospitalities," evaded grappling with what, among the old Corporations, was considered the giant abuse of them all,—the Corporation of London. Who, in such matters as the management of our roads, the lighting of towns, and water supply, have surrendered the national interests to a multitude of private Companies set on foot by the share market, and helped to ruin them by an augmentation of preliminary and parliamentary expenses before unheard of ; from which, and the mischievous action of monopolies, the public will have to suffer for generations to come. Who have so legislated for Insolvency as to have left us with no remedy and no punishment for fraudulent debt. Who, on the vital question of National Education, have gone back from the principles of the Commission of 1828, which recommended, and afterwards (in 1831) carried out for Ireland, " a system of combined literary and separate religious instruction," and have for England, substituted a voluntary Church and Denominational Scheme, founded on the principle that " to him that hath shall be given, and he shall have abundance, and from him that hath not shall be taken even that which he hath ; "the practical result being that out of 13,838 parishes in England, only 7,137, and those the richest, receive assistance from the Government grants ; while the 6,701 unaided poorer parishes, chiefly agricultural, are obliged to contribute (through the taxes) to the funds voted.† Who, with the better example

* Addenda 2.   † Ibid 3.

of Scotland before them, have shut their eyes to the fact that the great defect of this scheme is the enlarging of Church patronage, and the strengthening of sectarian distinctions; with so low a minimum of instructional benefit to the people, that to this very day one-third the women of England and one-fourth the men of England are found unable to sign their names to a marriage register!*

True it is that many Liberal measures, including measures of a neutral complexion as regards party distinctions, have been passed since the Reform Act of 1832: (strange it would be if there had been absolutely no progress;) but looking through the whole of them,—Poor Law Amendment, Municipal reforms (such as they were), Registration of births, deaths, and marriages, Dissenters Marriage Bill, Penny Postage, Tithe Commutation Act, Improved Charity administration, District Union Schools, Repeal of Corn Laws, Repeal of Taxes on Knowledge, &c., I can discover no one among them that might not have been wrung, with a corresponding amount of agitation, from the Unreformed Parliament of 1831, or of which either the origin or the success can be distinctly traced to the subsequent enfranchisement of the more than a million of occupiers we then added to the register. The Reform Act helped forward those measures just so far only and no farther, that it placed electoral power in the hands of men who understood them; and it obstructed those measures to the full extent that it threw open the doors of Parliament to public-house and oyster-barrel candidates for admission. Whether on some points the balance of loss and gain may not have been favourable to the Liberal interest is perhaps doubtful, but Educationists, at least, should take warning that it has been notably adverse on all Church questions. The right of the State to appoint a Lay Inspector of Primary Schools in connection with the Church of England, when aided by public-money, has been abandoned for England and Wales. (The present 42 Inspectors of the so-called "National Schools" are all clergymen.) The Irish Church grievance has remained exactly as it stood in 1835; and no stand against Ecclesias-

* See Addenda 4.

tical encroachments on Civil Liberty, worth speaking of, has been made by our legislators since 1829, when an *unreformed* House of Commons, under the ministry of the Duke of Wellington, carried, in the teeth of clerical opposition, the great measure of Catholic Emancipation.

No my friend, no ; a thousand times no! If you want a champion of the Protestant right of private judgment, or of collegiate and scholastical emancipation from the *odium theologicum*, it is not to the ranks of the ignorant and dependent you must look for his support. They will be found, more frequently than not, submitting to be used as the tools of his enemies, denouncing and persecuting him perhaps for infidelity ; as in the case of Dr. Priestley, whose house, books, manuscripts, and philosophical apparatus, were destroyed by the populace of Birmingham, in 1791 ; a case of which we were reminded the other day, by the equally disgraceful Popery and No-Popery riots of June 16th and 17th in the same town; and corresponding with the reactionary influences we have seen in Italy, since the exploits of Garibaldi, in the seizure of Palermo by a monk led Sicilian peasantry ; and in the defeat of Garibaldi and his party of the Left, in the election of March 1867, in Florence, at Bologna, at Milan, and even in eleven out of the twelve colleges of Naples.

This latter reverse some reformers are trying to persuade themselves is owing to the new constitution of Italy not being yet sufficiently democratic. Never was there a greater mistake. A distrust of Garibaldi's prudence contributed, but the marked character of his defeat was due to the influence of the priesthood ; which although, in Italy, *nil* with the educated few, is still overpowering with the many, even among the personal admirers of the

* The present struggle in Italy is for a more rational disposal of a fund of £80,000,000 sterling, held by the Roman Catholic clergy, and largely misapplied. It is mere childishness to suppose, that those who have wielded for centuries this money power, should, aided by ignorance and superstition, have no influence with the multitude.

man. The Court of Rome would desire nothing better at the present moment than permission to place on the electoral register the agricultural labouring population of Calabria and the Abruzzi.

Nothing better than the success of the revolution of Belgium was desired, in 1830, by the Roman Catholic clergy of the latter country, while under the government of the Kingdom of the Netherlands; and its immediate results on the interests of education in Belgium were disastrous. The admirable system of popular instruction, which the Dutch government had inaugurated, was at once abolished. The priesthood, as advocates of " liberty of instruction," recovered the ascendency in the primary schools, and again left them to ruin. The same disaster would overtake our Irish schools, if a mandate from the Pope were to render possible, as it might do, with foreign assistance, at any moment, the success of a Fenian insurrection. Who could assert that the Irish Cottier, such as we see him, would not side with his priest, on any question connected with spiritual instruction, against the best orators of the Reform League ?

The classical student reads of the ostracism of Aristides the Just, and the English scholar of the Stuarts, recalled by a fickle and mis-guided people, aided by the soldiers of Monk, after the able administration of a Cromwell, to disgrace the country by the most corrupt court,—that of Charles II., England had ever seen ; but we have had, in our own time, a significant instance of the kind of response to be expected from direct appeals to ignorant masses, which should suffice at least for all reformers, of the present century, with republican aspirations. I allude to the election for President of the late French Republic, in December 1848 ; within six months, only, of General Cavaignac having become the hero of the middle classes, as the restorer of public order, by his suppression of the sanguinary *" Insurrection des ouvrières."* The votes were :—

M. Louis Napoleon	5,534,520
General Cavaignac	1,448,302
M. Ledru-Rollin	370,119
M. Raspail	36,900
M. Lamartine	17,910
General Changarnier	4,790

The test was a decisive one, for although, in subsequent French elections, questions have been raised of a tampering with the ballot-box, here there were none. The prefects of the departments were, then, all of Republican appointment ; and the ballot-boxes were therefore in the hands of the friends of Cavaignac. He had the support of all the true Liberalism and intelligence of France; but against him were united the physical-force men of the Trade Unions, the whole body of the Roman Catholic clergy, and a Peasantry so hopelessly ignorant, as to believe, in a multitude of cases, that they were voting, not for a stranger, whose good and bad qualities were at that time wholly untried, but for the old Napoleon ; not dead, after all, but alive, and happily returned from St. Helena.

It is the misfortune of honest Radicalism, in its fervid denunciations of tyrants, to be unconscious of the source of tyrannical power. It does not pause to reflect that a tyrant could not trample on a people without help from the people ; or that he oppresses one section of a community only by the aid of another. As a single individual, a tyrant would be harmless enough; any half-dozen women would be stronger than he ; but behind him is always a hydra-headed monster—a multitude ready to do a tyrant's bidding, and to play, each in turn, a tyrant's part. Brutus strikes at Cæsar, forgetting that it was the cheers of Romans that fired Cæsar's ambition, and not foreseeing that Romans will avenge his death. William Tell reserves his second arrow for an Austrian Gesler; unconscious that in the events to follow, his own countrymen will play a leading part as "the mercenary Swiss," hired for the suppression of liberty in other lands. Much has often been said of the folly of the crowned heads of Europe, in ruining themselves and their subjects by immense standing armies, forming now an aggregate of two millions of men. The folly is great, but not so serious as the fact that there are always two millions of men, and more at their back, consenting to be so employed ; men, grumbling sometimes at conscriptions, but ready, without a question asked, at the command of a little Corporal, to put a bullet or a bayonet into any

Imperialism, with no pretence of popular suffrage about it ; in our free Colonies, in conflicts of races,—African, European, Indian, Chinese, and Polynesian, occasioning daily embarrassment ; and in England itself, in a political dead-lock, a Ministry appeared to whom the bright thought had occurred, as a revelation from heaven, that before legislating again for the construction of a new Constitution's edifice, it would be well to have a little preliminary discussion about its foundations.

Macaulay's New Zealander will learn from the debates of 1867, how such a proposal, made by Mr. Disraeli, was received;—by some as a device to gain time, and by the majority of our 658 statesmen as something so preposterously needless, that a smile, or a shout of ridicule, was its only answer. Democritus, were he now living, would smile or shout in his turn, while Heraclitus would weep, over the abundant demonstration that has since been given of the impossibility of any permanent settlement of the Reform question, without a better knowledge of First Principles than prevailed, in and out of Parliament, at the opening of the session.

Its fruits have been another political compromise ; fairly, and frankly characterised by the Minister driven to it as " a leap in the dark ;" and I pass on, omitting, to avoid prolixity, much that, here, should otherwise be said, to sketch, as briefly as possible, the conditions under which the leap is taken. A leap in the dark it is, not only to Lord Derby, but to most of his usual opponents ; to some of whom, the broad day light that is coming, may bring astonishment, and self-reproach.

30 & 31 Vict., cap. 102.

1. The preamble of the new Act states it to be " expedient to amend the laws relating to the representation of the people;" and its provisions assume, generally, that the way to amend those laws is to extend the Suffrage.

2. The Suffrage is a share in the National Government, which may, of course, be extended either to right or to wrong parties, and be distributed in right or in wrong proportions. It may be partial or

universal, equal or unequal, direct or indirect. *Universal* Suffrage, as was long ago pointed out by Horne Tooke, is one thing, and *Equal* Universal Suffrage is another. The new Act is an advance, and a very considerable one, towards Direct and *Equal* Universal Suffrage; with a view to which it provides for a general lowering of electoral qualifications.

8. In lowering electoral qualifications the Act sets aside all considerations of moral or intellectual fitness for the electoral duty to be discharged. It goes at once down to the class in the lowest state of cultivation, and reduces the highest to the same level. There is to be no recognition of grades of merit as connected with citizenship, so that a vote, or an additional power of voting, might be earned as an honourable distinction. Property is to be dissevered from the franchise, or nearly so, and education, experience, character, talent, are not to take its place. A Civil Service examination for India, tasks, in the severest manner, every power of the mind, but those who are to vote for the rulers of India may never have heard of its existence. The Act, it is probable, enfranchises fully half-a-million persons unable to read and write; and this not by an inadvertence, for it was settled by the House of Commons that reading and writing were not necessary to an intelligent electoral act! The proposal of Lord Lyttleton, (July 80th,) that electors should at least be able to write a hand sufficiently legible for a signature was, in the Upper House, met with a jest about the bad handwriting of noble Lords, and also negatived.

The only exception to this legislation in favour of ignorance, (for, in deference to the views of popular leaders all " Fancy Franchises " have been swept away,) is a clause (25) for partially extending the old Parliamentary privileges of Oxford, Cambridge, and Dublin Universities, and of such of their old graduates as can afford, after leaving, to keep on the rolls by continued payment of heavy College fees, to the London University. " Every man whose name is, for the time being, on the Register of Graduates constituting the Convocation" of the latter, will now have the privilege of voting for a member; but for one member only.

4. In reference to property qualifications for the Suffrage, the tendency of the Act is towards their total abolition. The minimum laid down for that stake in the country which every one should possess before he takes part in the administration of its resources, may almost be described as the invisible point of metaphysicians, —that which constitutes the ultimate difference between something and nothing. The new Franchise, for Boroughs, is, nominally, Household Suffrage; which, as understood by old reformers, had always a respectable sound; but, as defined by the new Act, should be called simply Occupancy Suffrage; for the holder of a house shut up, (although requiring protection for it, and always liable for some portion of the local burdens,) is not, by the Act, admitted to be a householder; while it is only by a misnomer that the long rows of miserable two-room tenements and broken down hovels, which disfigure the outskirts of many of our towns can be called " houses." The Act goes out of its way to include all such structures by abolishing (clause 7) the custom (called compounding,) of assessing them in the name of the owner. " The full rateable value of every dwelling-house, *or other separate tenement*," is now to be entered in the rate-book, with the name of the occupier, in order that its occupier (instead of the owner) may be enfranchised. Every hut, thatched cottage, and mud cabin in any Borough of England and Wales is embraced in the category; and the tub of Diogenes, entered at " its full rateable value," would be a house within the meaning of the Act.

Recognising and allowing, paternally, for the penury of this class of occupiers, the Act provides that their rate qualification shall be limited to the payment of any poor rate levied during six months. Payment of no other rate or tax is necessary to the vote. An amendment by the Lords which would have involved equal liability to Borough and County rates, was rejected by the Commons. On which the question should have been asked, how, in such case, the right of the Tenement occupier to influence, even remotely, the distribution of Borough and County rate funds, can ever arise; and how, especially, his right can be established to affect by a vote the parliamentary disposal of a house duty, seeing that no house duty is ever levied on tenements.

The new Act gives no reasons, but enacts that any man, not on the parish, who may have obtained, rent free, from the kindness of neighbours, the twelvemonth's shelter of four walls, assessed perhaps at a value of ten shillings per annum, and can command, towards an election time, the few pence only of a poor rate which could be levied on such premises between January and July, shall be entitled to the franchise.

To working men of a higher status, living in decent lodgings, the Act refuses the franchise, unless their lodgings, unfurnished, be equal to the value of £10 per annum. It will not therefore escape the notice of societies for the erection of improved dwelling houses for the poor, that the Act is, *pro tanto*, much less favourable to their objects than to the multiplication of tiled sheds. A cheap Tenement suffrage offers, obviously, over again, the same facilities for the creation of fagot votes as existed in the days of Pocket boroughs. History repeats itself, and we are in the hands of those of whom, although of different parties, it will be said, as of the elder Bourbons,— " they had forgotten nothing, and learned nothing."

5. The Lodger franchise, in Boroughs, of ten pounds per annum, or four shillings per week, is to be without rate-paying; on the principle that rates are always, more or less, counted in the rent; a fact, but one which, if supplying a suitable rule for a line of suffrage demarcation, should exempt all classes of tenant voters from the necessity of direct rate-paying. The minimum qualification for a County vote is now reduced to the occupancy, for a year, with rate paying, of any land or tenement of the rateable value of twelve pounds per annum; that is, of five shillings per week ; or, with rates added, about six shillings per week.

6. These qualifications are, perhaps, sufficiently low to place on the register a clear numerical majority of the wages class of the population ; which, however, if numbers alone did not govern,

would not be in itself a ground for uneasiness. That the wages class should have their fair share of political power is not to be denied; the question for sober consideration is, whether if we transfer to a simple majority of this class the whole political power of the country, we give them their fair share, or more than their fair share. Are we quite prepared to reduce, by a system combining, with extension, *equal* voting and an *equal* distribution of voting power, the holders of capital, as well as the possessors of superior knowledge, to simple units ?

The principle of equal voting, in the case of persons not of equal standing, is that one-sided equality, which no one accepts in his own private business transactions; which is wholly at variance with the laws of commercial partnership; and which has never, hitherto, been admitted into the British Constitution without counteracting checks, more or less efficient, but often clumsily applied. The reason four members were given to the City of London, while two only were assigned to a County, with a much greater population, was that anciently the City was held to represent the greater wealth and intelligence;—a sound reason, although not one for allowing, individually, in these times, the same power of voting to a City waterman, or " 'long shoreman," as to a City banker.

Mr. J. S. Mill, when he proposed to place all such plurality of voting on a common-sense footing,* was treated as an innovator; so was Mr. Disraeli, when he asked only to qualify his extensions with a dual vote in certain cases; but the greatest innovators on established customs,—the oldest customs of mankind, as affecting property, are those now seeking to do away with a variable suffrage power altogether; and the precedent they are chiefly following is the comparatively modern one of the Municipal Reform Act of 1835.

The equal voting powers conferred by the Reform extensions of 1832 were mostly confined to an equal class,—the middle class; but the Municipal Reform Act had to deal with ratepayers of all classes, and it fell unhappily under the influence of men misled by the fallacy which Horne Tooke had exposed,† or dishonestly

* See Addenda, 5.   † Ibid 6.

seeking to make political capital by it,—the fallacy of the cry that
"the poor man's penny is equal to the rich man's pound." Under
the provisions therefore of the 5th and 6th Will. IV. c. 76, which all
but treats ownership as an offence, penny ratepayers (and by the
13 and 14 Vict. c. 99, Small Tenement occupiers, not even paying
their penny directly, but only through compounding landlords,)
have been permitted to do as they pleased with rich men's pounds,
until the condition of many of our new Corporations is known to be
worse than that of the old.—Bribery at municipal elections, with a view
to local jobbing, (as at New York,) is now again the rule rather than
the exception,* and to check that fraudulent dealing with Corporate
estates through which we have sometimes seen even a Town Hall seized
by creditors, an Act has had to be passed (23 Vict. c. 6) to give an
optional veto on the proceedings of Town Councils, in matters
relating to transfers and mortgages, to the Lords of the Treasury.

7.   The untrustworthiness of our Municipal constituencies, from the
preponderance of power given by equal voting to small and temporary interests over larger and fixed interests, is a calamity in itself;
but doubly a misfortune at the present time, as tending to per-
petuate that over-centralisation of public business in the House
of Commons, which is really the great national grievance for which a
change in our social organisation is most required.

The House of Commons is a body, which with 658 members,
undertook, thirty-five years back, to discharge all the legislative
duties required for a population of twenty-four millions; it now
undertakes, without any new coadjutors, the same functions for
thirty millions; the theory of the new Act being that, for a General
Council, 658 is a perfect number; which for some reasons of mystery,
or magic, peculiar to the wise men of this country, and not certainly
derived from those of the East,† should not be changed for a single

---

* See Addenda, 7.

† The Council of Nice was composed of but 318 members;—the number
of Abraham's servants, and that contained in the Greek letters for Helios,
the Sun.

figure, more or less. That it should not be changed for larger figures, while all Parliamentary business is transacted under one roof, is plain enough, since when the whole 658 are assembled they are seen to form, necessarily, a disorderly crowd; but on the other hand the duties now devolving on this body are overwhelming; or would be so, if, practically, apart from field-day conflicts, it were anything more than a Registration Court, for work really done by Government clerks. Three Acts of Parliament a day, or 485 for the Session,—122 public, and 363 local, were the measures the House had to get through, in some fashion, in 1866. And why, it may be asked, for such minor objects of legislation, as were embraced by the latter, and might be styled Provincial, should there not be more than one House of Commons, or competent representative body, assembling, (where such matters would be better understood, and could be more fully discussed,) in other centres of activity than the metropolis.

8. And this leads me to remark that a fundamental error has been committed on all sides by agreeing, in our late discussions, to a dislocation of this question, by dividing it into three parts; as if a reform of Parliament did not concern the United Kingdom, but only the two provinces of England and Wales.

The new Reform Act does not include Scotland and Ireland. Separate bills are to be introduced for these provinces, or ancient kingdoms, next Session. So that the battle is not yet half fought out; for the time is surely past when it can be contended that an Irishman or Scotchman should be treated either as a conquered enemy or as an inferior animal, *per se*, to an Englishman. Whatever share of suffrage power is to be, in 1869, the privilege of an intelligent and wealthy Englishman should, plainly, be the right of any equally intelligent and wealthy Scotchman or Irishman; and to the precise extent that we have now given a direct and equal vote with the best in the land to the lowest class of Englishmen, we, next Session, must be prepared to admit the claims of the Scotch Highlander, and the

Irish Cottier. The following, in reference to them, shows, approximately, our present position.

	Area in Statute Acres.	Estimated Population in 1867.	Registered Electors.	Members.
England and Wales	37,094,400	21,300,000	1,100,000	500
Scotland..........	19,738,930	8,200,000	105,000	53
Ireland	19,441,944	5,600,000	205,000	105
	76,275,274*	30,100,000	1,410,000	658

If, for our renewed starting point, we take 500 as the proper number of members to represent two-thirds of a population of 30,000,000, then by the laws of arithmetic and every rule of logic, 750, and not 658, is the proper number for the whole; or that required for the United Kingdom. And, so far, the problem of Representation is sufficiently simple. Any child could draw up a Reform Bill, if we are simply to count heads, and not at all trouble ourselves about the limits of localisation and centralisation, or any adjustment of private interests, and abandon altogether the principle of a differential franchise.

9. The authors of the new Act are not prepared to go quite this length, although making a prodigious stride in that direction; they are still for retaining differential franchises where wrong reasons can be assigned for them, and refuse them only when asked for on right grounds. The voting power conferred by such a building as the Charing Cross Hotel, is, for a Borough, one with that of a tenement in any mews at the back; but a difference is recognised between Borough and Borough, and Borough and County; as if Representation concerned places, alone, and not the interest of their inhabitants.

10. The new Act reduces the suffrage power of fifty-eight small Boroughs, at present returning 116 members, one half; abolishes it altogether (for corruption) in the case of four Boroughs returning

* Exclusive of British Island, Isle of Man, Guernsey, Jersey, &c., 1,119,159 acres. For further details of Population, see Addenda, 8.

7 members; and distributes the 65 members thus unseated over certain of the old and other new constituencies. Not so as to do away with disparities, but so as to retain them, on a broader basis ; all constituencies now to comprise greater numbers, but, relatively to each other, to be much the same as before ; some large and some small; some returning one member, others two members, others three members, and the City of London four members.

The principle of such an arrangement is unintelligible, for what has the franchise of an individual elector to do with his choice to live in a crowd or in a solitude ? Will it, now, be an act of greater virtue to reside in the new Borough of Chelsea, which is to return two members, than in Guildford, which is to return but one ? It would seem so ; for if a virtuous elector of Chelsea commit the indiscretion of removing to Guildford he will lose a vote !

11. The new Act, to avoid meeting fairly the question of property qualifications, repeats the blunder of the old Reform Act, (made innocently, with the object only of excluding nominal burgesses), in restricting the Borough franchise to residents; however large and *bona-fide* the interest of the non-resident; and sanctions again the inconsistency of allowing, for counties, the franchise to a 40s. freeholder, without any restriction as to residency ;—another striking illustration of a differential franchise retained on a false basis : and, connected with it, is one still more absurdly wrong-headed.

12. A landlord millionnaire, if his whole property be derived from ground rents in a single county, has but two votes to represent it,—that is, a vote for two members ; but if he, or a less wealthy man, buy up 40s. freeholds in different counties, he is allowed to gain two votes for every county in which he thus becomes interested ; and practically, at the present moment, many county electors hold a plurality of votes in this form, affecting the return of twenty or thirty members.

13. Disparities of size in constituencies create another kind of differential franchise equally illogical, as tending only to defeat its proper end. Thus the registered electors of Ipswich, returning two members, are at the present moment, 2,118. The registered

electors of Finsbury, also returning two members, are 25,461. The suffrage power, therefore, of Ipswich, is twelve times greater than that of Finsbury. A difference which could only be justified by the old Sacerdotal theory about Holy places, alluded to, which held it to be more meritorious to live in Jerusalem than Jericho; or on the assumption that the aggregate intelligence and property of the Ipswich electors is twelve times greater than that of the Finsbury electors. Whether the new Reform Act will make any change in these proportions will depend on the accident of there being possibly more Small Tenement occupiers, and 4s. a week lodgers in one place than the other. If there be no more, and if the constituency of each place should say simply be doubled, at the next general election, the inequality of their respective shares in the Representation will remain the same. The new Act, however, it is probable, will introduce many greater disparities than now prevail between constituency and constituency; small tenements, low rented houses, and houses let in lodgings not being equally scattered over the country. It may be expected that some boroughs will be enlarged but slightly, and others five fold. The electors of Calne are now 174; of Thetford 224; of Knaresborough 272; of Wells 274; and the new average of these and corresponding quiet market towns may, perhaps, not exceed 1,000, while that of others, at present on a par with them, may be raised to 5,000 or 10,000; and we must not be surprised to see constituencies approaching 100,000.

14. There will be a limit to this, in the circumstance that a sliding scale of extension is at the same time a sliding scale of indifference. An elector values his privilege when it enables him to act where every vote tells, but when he is obliged to share it with so many thousands that, all voting, the influence of a single vote on the result of an election is quite inappreciable, he is apt very soon to regard the privilege as of little account. Under the new Reform Act, therefore, multitudes, duly qualified, will not claim to be placed on the register. This we may be sure of, because, in our largest constituencies, at the present moment, it is rare that more than half the number already placed there can, at contested

elections, be brought to the poll. And unhappily those who stay away from indifference are not, usually, the persons whose assistance at a poll could, by honest men, be best dispensed with. Electors still more indifferent about voting, but who, as far as a vote itself is concerned, value the thing for what it will bring, even if it bring nothing more than payment of a beer score, are certain to be at their post; kept up to it, when necessary, by a professional election agent, who, to refresh his own memory, has all their names alphabetically arranged in his office ledgers, with algebraical signs attached.

The operation of this law of human nature, in large constituencies, is often to transfer power from the majority to a minority, and that a minority, not composed of the best elements of a community, but of its worst. This is the evil already working in our Metropolitan Boroughs, the mischiefs of which the new Reform Act must greatly aggravate. Take, for illustration, the case of a silk merchant, and that of some neighbouring publican supported by the prize ring. The silk merchant, finding his individual share of the suffrage power now more insignificant than before, will, it is probable, more frequently than before, abstain from voting, or from claiming to vote. Not so the publican; for a person of his class, whether an honest or a dishonest man, becomes, under the new Act, from his position, as a central point of union for voters having no other, the most influential member of British Society.

15. A peculiar tendency in our electoral arrangements to discourage the better class of electors from exercising their privileges, and practically therefore to create a differential suffrage in favour of an inferior class, has long existed, and by the new Act is to continue to exist, in the requirement, for voting, of personal attendance. By the better class of voters I do not mean the wealthiest, but the most active, industrious, and intelligent; who are, necessarily, the busiest members of a community, and therefore the persons to whom personal attendance at a distance, on a given day, not of their own appointment, is often an impossibility, and always involves a sacrifice. A civil engineer may be wanted in Edinburgh when he

should be voting in London; a railway guard on the day of election has to accompany a through train from London to York; a commercial traveller is thrown out of a gig; a surgeon from the nearest town, perhaps ten miles off, is summoned to attend him; judge, jury, counsel, witnesses, are shut up in a Criminal Court from 10 till 6; and the whole of these lose their votes; while voters out of work, or out on strike, or fortunately engaged just at that time by "the man in the moon" on moonshine avocations, find personal attendance no inconvenience, and are thus made masters of the situation.

In 1861 this foolish restriction was relaxed in favour of Oxford, Cambridge, and Dublin Universities by the Act of 24 aud 25 Vict., c. 53, which allows for those bodies the convenience of voting papers;* and the new Act, therefore, by clause 45, extends the same privilege to the University of London. The clauses, however, introduced by the Lords† in the original Bill, for allowing voting papers to all who cared to claim them, were disagreed to by the Commons,§ and to avoid a collision of the two Houses, finally withdrawn.

They embraced a complicated system of checks, that would practically have been very costly and troublesome in the working, to meet the case of electors not able to read what they sign, or to sign any thing, except with a mark; and the expediency of attempting at all to adapt voting papers to such a difficulty, could not be very clearly made out. We may offer a pen to a man who can write, as we lend a horse to him who can ride; but we

---

* For the form of voting paper, see Addenda, 9.

† August 2nd. On the motion of the Marquis of Salisbury:—

For voting papers..	114
Against „	36
Majority........	78

§ August 8th. On the question that the House disagree with the Lords' Amendment :—

For	258
Against ....:..	206
Majority against voting papers..	52

may wisely withhold the pen where it must be guided by the hand of another, as we refuse a horse, even to a friend, whose want of horsemanship might, if we permitted him to mount, cause him to break his neck.

This is so plain, that the propriety of such distinctions of suffrage as would at least allow, by different forms of voting, the ignorant to remain where they are, and the educated to enjoy the privileges of education, must ultimately be admitted. We tolerate powers of attorney, dock warrants, railway transfers, affidavits affecting property to any amount, and concerning matters even of life and death, to be enclosed in a letter and transmitted by post; and we have got so far as to allow a B.A. or an M.A. at the Lakes, to give his opinion on the fitness of Mr. Gladstone to sit in parliament without a special journey to Oxford. The time cannot be distant when we shall sanction the absence from an election of a physician, watching by the bedside of the dying, without subjecting him to the penalty of disfranchisement.

A great enlargement of the suffrage is itself a reason for dispensing with personal attendance at elections, to the full extent that it can be safely done, because, where there is a dense population, personal attendance means the collection of crowds, and crowds collision. This should be especially accepted as a reason in favour of voting papers by all friends of Female Suffrage;—a question which can hardly make serious progress without them.

16. The new Act renews the old suffrage disabilities of the sex. A rich man dies, leaving his estates to his widow. She administers them carefully, pays all rates and taxes upon them, builds schools, founds charities, enlarges churches, but is held to be disqualified by nature from either representing others, or being herself represented. Yet how is this? The British Constitution knows nothing of the anomaly. A woman sits upon the throne; women are recognised as parishioners, vote in open vestries, act as overseers; and women, among aboriginal tribes are often found sitting at the Council Board. How is it that in countries blest with what is

D

called Representative Government woman seems, in this respect,
to have lost caste, or to have slipped from her original station of
companionship, as the helpmeet of man?

The reason is honourable to womanhood. In those softening and
refining influences which belong to the noblest attributes of mind,
and which "Auld Nature" found wanting, after " Her 'prentice
han' she tried on man," Woman has not failed in her leadership,
but, in the march of true civilisation, is still in advance of
her lord. Whether originally taken from his side or not, she
now shrinks from the Gorilla who would force her back to the banks
of his native Gaboon. The public, a few years back, saw, not with
displeasure, but with much satisfaction, Miss Nightingale take her
place at the head of a military hospital staff; but what if that good
angel of the Crimean soldier could only have entered upon her
mission of humanity through the electoral forms insisted upon for
candidates by the rougher partisans of an exclusively Manhood
Suffrage! Who can imagine her meeting, with amiable smiles, a
canvassing committee at the Red Lion, or Pig and Thistle, or
escorted by banner men, winding her way through the fustian-jacket
bearers of knobsticks to gain the planks and sawdust of a fair-booth
hustings; and, there, pitching her voice to a scream, and straining it
till red in the face, after the manner of our Hyde Park rhetoricians,
to deliver an address, which nobody can hear, from the noise made
by idlers pelting each other, for amusement, with cabbage stalks, or
by rioters creating intentional disturbance? Instinctively every
woman feels that in such scenes she can take no part. Instinctively
the public mind revolts against her doing so; and although prejudice
against a female suffrage is now beginning somewhat to yield to
reason,* never shall we see it wholly overcome, and woman consulted,

---

* It was satisfactory to see that the minority on Mr. Mill's motion of May
20th for omitting the word man, and substituting the word person, was much
greater than expected. .

For retaining the word man	196
For substituting the word person..............	73

Majority against Female Suffrage   123

legislatively, when she should be, on all questions affecting, peculiarly, the interest of her own sex, and often immediately concerning the happiness of both sexes, until the whole machinery of Rowdyism is separated from Representation.

17. A small step, but a small one only, towards that end, and with the general aim of some partial alleviation of the inconvenience of personal attendance at elections, is made by clauses 34 and 37, which give permission to a returning officer to hire rooms, for polling places, where they can be obtained, (usually only at public houses,) instead of erecting booths; and direct him to provide for such an increased number "as would enable each voter, as far as practicable, to have a polling place within a convenient distance of his residence."

An increased number of polling places, with a staff of officers and clerks at each polling place, will be a very expensive substitute for voting papers, and their cost out of all proportion to the accommodation they will afford. A London barrister, on the York Circuit, will derive little advantage from the privilege of polling at the Prince and Feathers, within a stone's-throw of his villa at Dulwich ; and we may assume as a general rule for what an elector may call his *residence*, because the abode where his wife and children sleep at night, that it is the place of all others in which it is least convenient for him to be present during the day. If we want to find a man, of any activity of mind or body, in what are called business hours, we seek him in his office, his counting house, his shop, his club, his farm, his factory, but not at his private house ; knowing that there, unless laid up from illness, we should certainly *not* meet with him. A glimmering perception of this fact has led to an extension, in clause 46, of the area of residence for citizens of London from seven miles to twenty-five; but a City Alderman living at Croydon or Hornchurch, will not on that account require more polling places. His most convenient centre will still be Guildhall.

18. "Residency" and "Occupancy" are terms belonging to an ancient cobweb of ideas, about the objects of an electoral registration,

which it is high time to sweep from our minds. A revising barrister ought to be concerned with but two classes of claims:—those belonging to personal qualifications, and claims derived from property. If we give a poor man a vote, either because 21 years of age, or for some better reason, as that he may be 45, the head of a family, a superior scholar, or a man who has obtained, for brave and honourable conduct, a Victoria Cross, we do not want to know anything more of his "residence" or "occupancy" than his address on the day of registration. If a soldier or sailor, we know beforehand that he has no fixed place of abode. If we agree that for the protection of capital,—the fruits of industry, property should share in the representation, then an electoral register should show what the property in a district is; distinguishing the owners, as the owners of leases, the owners of freeholds, the owners of stock in trade, owners and joint owners of mines, docks, railways, canals, &c., and giving the names of the agents through whom, when absent, the owners act. Residency, or occupancy is, here, again quite beside the question. A man who sinks a well or builds a factory chimney does not intend to live in either; but wherever he has improved or created a property which can be seized for his debts, he should be held to be sufficiently "abiding" for suffrage purposes; abiding in spirit, if not in the flesh, "for where the treasure is, there will the heart be also."

19. An element of good, as connected with the question of the proper relations of majorities and minorities, which, if fully carried out, would of itself greatly diminish, if not wholly abate the disorders of elections, was introduced into the new Act, at the last moment. It appears in clause 9, which provides "that where constituencies return three members an individual elector shall vote but for two only."*

* Moved by Lord Cairns, August 30th, 1867:—

For the Clause	142
Against it	51
	91

See, also, Addenda, 12.

The principle is that no representation can be worthy of the name of a National Representation, which does not embrace a proportionate return of all the parties and interests of which a nation may be composed; opposed, of course, to that of a mere party leader, whose *beau ideal* of a House of Commons is that of a body exclusively composed of pledged partisans, with himself at the head.

A National Council, properly so called, would be a body of honest men meeting to consult, and to decide nothing without consulting; and it would be composed, as a nation is composed, not of persons wholly of one or of two shades of opinion, but of many different shades; of minorities, therefore, as well as majorities, and of minorities comprising the views and interests of a third, fifth, and even of a tenth section of a community, with those of its larger sections. If this principle, with that of an equitable differential suffrage, were so carried out that while a majority of votes would command the greater share of the representation, a tenth portion of them would also insure a tenth share, the present character of our elections would be wholly changed. They would lose that fierceness which belongs to every struggle in which the stakes are "all or none." The better class of electors could take part in them, without risk of utter defeat. The corrupt could never win a perfect triumph.

The best working method for such representation of minorities is a question admitting of much discussion, and this clause of the Lords, bearing upon it, will affect but slight improvement in the general operation of the present measure, but its adoption may be noticed as a sign of progress, of some promise for the future.

20. Towards that purification of constituencies, which, with the substitution of better elements, instead of a general lowering of qualifications, should now, after the experience we have had, have been the essential feature of a new Reform Act, the present Act offers us "a halfpenny-worth of bread" in the sentence it passes (12) on four constituencies out of our three hundred and seventy-four,—those of Totnes, Reigate, Great Yarmouth, and Lancaster.

Certain persons belonging to these Boroughs, named in the Schedules of the several reports of the Commission of Inquiry, as having been guilty of bribery, or receiving bribes, in all 2,035,* are visited with the penalty of disfranchisement, for town and county; and, so far, so good; but as there were fair grounds for presuming that others were equally guilty, not to be easily separated from the innocent, our legislators, to make a better show of doing something, have adopted the old device of punishing the innocent and guilty together; and so have deprived the whole of the inhabitants of these places of their right of suffrage, as far as it affected their Borough franchise. Totnes is a small place, but, for wealth and population Reigate, Great Yarmouth, and Lancaster, stand much above many boroughs permitted under the new Act to return a member. The aggregate population of the four is 64,791; their registered electors 4,412; and no one can believe either that the whole of the 4,412 were corrupt,† or that the greater number were worse than the majority of the rest of the 1,350,000 registered electors of Great Britain and Ireland, accustomed to accept from candidates, as commonly believed, £2,000,000 sterling every general election; and yet amongst whom our legislators have been unable to discover spot or speck.

If the inquiries of the Commissioners had extended from Great Yarmouth to Norwich, would their report have been more flattering to the latter than to the former? And if they had given us, with the names of the persons bribed in Great Yarmouth, full particulars

---

* Addenda, 10.

† Let me say for Reigate, of which I have some knowledge, that it contained at least one man whose moral worth should, alone, have saved it from the injustice of this indiscriminating stigma;—Thomas Martin, F.R.C.S., who, after a long life of usefulness, died February 12th, 1867, in his 88th year:—a pure minded philanthropist, worthy of a statue;—active and often foremost in every good work; unwearied in well-doing; patient; forgiving: one of the excellent of the earth. I owe to him a debt of gratitude for an example which has often helped to strengthen my faith in human nature, when much shaken.

of their station in life, as in their report for Lancaster, would it now be satisfactory to learn from the Clerk to the Norwich Board of Guardians, that the new Act has raised the number of assessments in Norwich, by the abolition of compounding, from 7,158 to 21,270?

Looking at the whole matter, commercially, and with a view solely to professional interests, the new Act may be regarded favourably, as opening a vastly increased field for the industrial activity of solicitors, barristers, surveyors, secretaries of registration societies, and election agents. The latter especially, now more indispensable than ever, will, if not belonging to the scrupulous, have abundant reason for self-congratulation, and will, at once, be able to dispel the fears of a wealthy client that the judicious application of ten or fifteen thousand pounds, on the eve of a contest, would not give him a better chance of success than another man. They are shrewd enough to perceive, what the public as yet do not, that in the larger boroughs, with the increased weight given to the mass, the personal influence of the class of electors, usually most inaccessible to canvassers, will, by equal voting, be greatly diminished ; that, as a general rule, the old voters, overwhelmed by the new, will retire from the field ; that a two hundred public house power will therefore be more irresistible than before ; that, in the smaller boroughs, a good business may still be done in the oyster barrel line, or in the discount of promissory notes for insolvent tradesmen ; and that, although the new Act makes fresh provisions against bribery, they will derive no support from public opinion, and will prove but another *brutum fulmen*.

A revolution has taken place in the public ethics, and we must learn to look it in the face. The soundness of the theory which affixes criminality to the sale and purchase of votes is denied. It is asked if, with the knowledge of the fact that Esau wishes to sell his birthright for a mess of pottage, our legislators deliberately, and with their eyes open, give him the power of doing so, why should we treat the exercise of that power, in the helplessness of his folly, as an offence ? Why drive him to the subterfuges that must add to folly the real crimes of hypocrisy and deceit? Is it of necessary consequence that the elector who accepts money for a vote must sin against light and knowledge? May he not sometimes have a defence unassailable by logic? Hear it:—"Two candidates have applied to me; a Whig and a Conservative. What the precise difference is between the one and the other, most sincerely, I do not know. Each has asked me to drink his health, and 'the ale is good on both sides.'* Here comes a third, of whom I know as little; he offers to lend me a five pound note when I want one. This is friendly, and with or without the ballot, I shall owe him a good turn."

And what is the defence of the briber? It is that the persons who accept money for the votes would, if it were not offered, still be morally disqualified from choosing a representative on higher grounds; and that the term bribe is therefore a misnomer for what should more correctly be described as the "black mail," which must be paid by all travellers who fall into the hands of thieves.

Very sad is the state of a country in which the validity of such a defence must to a large extent be admitted. The criminal classes of England and Wales, levying black mail in its simplest form, are estimated at 145,041.† Of the class that should be included with them, levying black mail through associations of the pattern of the Sheffield Saw-grinders' Union, we can have no returns; but we now see, from the evidence, that their victims paying it for protection, not against masters, but their own fellows, usurping a right to grant licenses for labour, must embrace a very considerable portion of our wages population. Nine and twenty years ago I stood at the bedside of a peasant in the Infirmary of Sligo,‡ who showed me his wrist with its sinews severed,—slashed to the bone, by a party of reapers,

---

* This, on one occasion, was the literal answer of a puzzled Staffordshire elector to the question,—"On which side do you vote?"

† Addenda, 11.

‡ James Doulan, visited September 26th, 1838. Two men held him down, while a third took away his sickle, and with it disabled him for life.

at whose bidding he had refused to strike; and now, after we had begun to believe in the assurance, that in England, at least, Terrorism connected with trade combinations had become extinct, we are startled by the discovery of its renewed development on a more gigantic scale than in former years.

In the milder form of fees and per centages to servants and others, the payment of black mail, in various disguises, is the sole condition on which a multitude of tradesmen are permitted to exist. Black mail, in various disguises, seats and unseats the members of our Town Councils and Boards of Guardians; and honest men are submitting to it, not in the interests of corruption, but as a wife submits to collect the ransom for her husband demanded by a captain of banditti:—as the only means left of resisting the open plundering of the public by jobbers, turning to their own account the weaknesses of ignorance and great need.

Do I write this without belief in, or sympathy for, those heroes of the humbler ranks, who have often take part in a Reform movement, and may be doing so at this present moment? Very far from it. I take from an old portfolio the full length portrait of one of them, upon which, for its speaking expression of conscious rectitude and sturdy independence, I have often looked with pleasure,—that of Robert Davies, tinman, of Wakefield; who, at the election for that borough, in July, 1837, refused a bribe of thirty pounds. But can we honestly say that in the framing of this new Reform Act there has been the slightest aim at distinguishing such men from the common crowd? Is it not rather true, and ominously true, that its bias is against them, and in favour of the advocates of the very doctrines preached by our ratteners and picketers,—those of a general Levelism?

A clause in the Act, which postpones its operation for a year, offers us a brief interval for reflection. Some advantage might be taken of it for a remission at least of the more mischievous of its provisions,—those relating to the compound householder. But where are the

Reform leaders to bid us halt back on a wrong road ? Apathy and despondency have seized upon the middle classes, recklessly resigning themselves to whatever may happen, as if overwhelmed with the gloom of some Stygian Lake, into which they had been thrown.

The words recall another of my old Reform reminiscences, with which it may be appropriate to conclude. It relates to John Thelwall, who, with Hardy and Horne Tooke, stood his trial for High Treason in 1794 ; a man of rare genius, and, for simple integrity, one of the worthiest of our old pioneers. For several years before his death, which happened in 1834, he had confined himself to teaching the art of elocution, of which he was a master ; and it was my privilege to hear one of his lectures, on that subject,— illustrative of Milton. I remember it, partly for the maxim which he took occasion, in speaking of pronunciation, to impress on the young men present, myself amongst the number, that it was better sometimes to be wrong with the educated, than right with the vulgar ; and for the power which, he taught us, might be given to language by a proper expression; of which, before, I had had but a feeble conception. The effect of his delivery of Satan's address to the fallen angels, was like an electric shock. It sent a thrill through me, which, after forty years, I feel still, as I try to imagine him standing at my side, (would that he were), repeating the same words, as he might now deliver them, in the sense, with some change of circumstances, of their present application:—

> "Princes, Potentates,
> Warriors, the flower of heaven once yours, now lost ;
> If such astonishment as this can seize
> Eternal spirits; or have ye chosen this place,
> After the toil of battle, to repose
> Your wearied virtue, for the ease you find
> To slumber here, as in the vales of heaven?
> Or in this abject posture have ye sworn,
> To adore the conqueror? — —
> Awake, arise, or be for ever fallen !"

                                        H.

September 8th, 1867.

ADDENDA.

1. *Public Expenditure.*

The charges for 1866-7 were :—

Army Services	£15,253,000
Naval Services	10,926,000
Civil Services	8,203,000
Revenue Department	5,045,000
Packet Services	807,000
	40,234,000
Interest on Debt	26,000,000
Charges on Consolidated Fund	1,900,000
	£68,134,000

In 1835, according to Porter's Tables, the following were the charges for—

Army	£6,406,143
Navy	4,099,430
Ordnance	1,151,914
	£11,657,487

The total expenditure for the same year was £45,669,309.

2. *Poor Rate for England and Wales.*

Date.	Population.	Total Levied.	Total Expended in Relief and Maintenance of Poor
1834	14,372,000	£8,338,079	£6,317,255
1844	16,410,000	6,847,205	4,976,093
1854	18,617,000	6,973,220	5,282,853
1864	20,663,000	9,448,319	6,243,381

The increase in the total amount of Poor Rate arises principally from " Payments for or towards the County, Hundred or Borough Rate, or Police Rate," which for 1864 were £2,163,290, for 1834 only £691,548.

	Mean number of able-bodied paupers (exclusive of vagrants) at one time in receipt of *in* and out-door relief.	Price of Wheat.
1854	135,191	61s. 7d. per Quarter.
1864	188,422	43s. 2d. ,,

3. *Educational Grants.*

" The Committee of Privy Council print a table corrected up to December 1866, showing the number of parishes in England grouped according to population, which do or do not contain schools aided with annual grants. From this it appears, first, that out of 13,838 parishes in England only 7,137, or little more than half,—receive aid from the State.

" The populous parishes can nearly always obtain assistance; it is in the small and of course rural parishes, that the great deficiency occurs. Of parishes with less than 500 inhabitants, less than one-eighth are aided. The number of the latter receiving grants is 924, the number receiving no grants s 7,295."—*Times,* July 19th, 1867.

4. *State of Popular Instruction.*

The annual reports of the Registrar General supply us with an infallible test of the actual progress of elementary instruction; of which it is only satisfactory to observe that it is not quite stationary. The Registrar observes that " *one* in *three* of the young men, and *one* in *two* of the young women of England could not write their names in the marriage register in 1841; while in 1864, but *one* in *four* of the men, and *one* in *three* of the women signed with marks.

During the twenty-three years the proportion in every hundred marriages, of marks-men has fallen from 33 to 23; of marks-women from 49 to 32.

Date.	Total Marriages in England.	Men who signed with marks.	Women who signed with marks.
1841	122,496	39,954	59,680
1864	147,914	41,998	58,402

The relative numbers of the ignorant to the instructed have diminished with the growth of the population, but the *absolute* numbers of the uneducated have undergone no diminution; and these figures, showing averages only, give no accurate idea of the neglected state of some parts of the country.

The Registrar General says (speaking of 1864):—" Of 100 men marrying, 90 could write their names in Westmoreland, 89 in London, 83 in Northumberland, 83 in the East Riding, 81 in the North Riding, 81 in Hants, 81 in Sussex, 80 in Cumberland, 80 in Devon. The proportion thus goes on descending deplorably from county to county until it falls to 63 in Bedford, Hertford, and South Wales, 62 in Stafford, and 58 in Monmouth. The excessive ignorance of the colliers of Staffordshire and Wales is a cause of incalculable evils, among others of explosions, and probably of strikes."

The Registrar contrasts this state of things with that of the counties round Aberdeen, where ninety-seven in every hundred marrying men, and ninety-one in every hundred women, wrote their names; and remarks (p. xviii.) that " it is difficult to explain a difference so creditable to Scotland in any other way than that, in the general struggle for the Church property at the Reformation, the people had the good sense to endow the schoolmasters with small stipends, and not to give the whole revenue of the land either to the clergy or to the nobility. Between the ministers and the lords stood the schoolmasters in the presence of the people."

In England we are making the schoolmaster more and more dependent on the minister, even for bread; and we lose our best teachers as fast as we gain them by leaving them without a career. A good schoolmaster cannot rise, without himself taking Holy Orders, because all Collegiate or other appointments connected with public instruction of the slightest value above those of a primary school, are allowed to be monopolised by the Clergy. The situation of a Government Inspector of Education (worth about £600 per annum), which for secular objects of instruction, at least, should have been especially reserved as a prize for secular teachers, of experience and merit, is converted into a new kind of Church living. This has arisen from the Government grants being principally distributed through a Society under the direct patronage of the Bench of Bishops, called the *National School Society*, and which may now be considered as, *de facto*, a branch of the Establishment. This Society stipulated as the condition of its co-operation, that all Inspectors for Schools in connection with it should be persons approved of by the Archbishops of Canterbury and York. The present total number of

Inspectors for Education is 54; 8 for ti
of Roman Catholics, and 42 for tho s
course, embrace generally with the
every body, non-sectarian. Among
all are clergymen; some of them, i
qualifications, but all, as a body.
of Sacerdotal Sovereignty whic!
with; and the tendency of whi
of the contracting operation
The members of the Clerica
in all Church formularies
duties, and are thus very g.
to be the best for citizens .
very summer of Reform a
bourhood of Blackheath, l
kept out of the sunshir
memory the whole of th
important of their schoo

Sir John Bowring, at
4th) observed:—" In (
step till his handwritin
Chinese there was not
When Governor of H
nected, with strong r
been brought to him
the word candle. II

5. *Plurality of*
" There is a wic
and acknowledging
counted for exactly
in the communi
equality, it would
so greatly outnu
labourer had
exercised min
ought to have
tion requires s
intellectual qu
or trader, wh
power of gui
should have
accurate, a
Thoughts on

6. *Equa*
Joh
reply
uni

R INQUIRERS.

BY

C. Hickson.

No. I.

REFORM.

jects of the work—Biographical notice of the
against the direction given to popular impulses
supporters of the Reform League—Reply to a letter,
ews, in the *Star*. An account of the *Insurrection des*
ris of 1848—Remarks upon the alliance of Free
de Union Protectionists.

LONDON:

...DGE & SONS, 5 PATERNOSTER ROW.

Price Sixpence.

a

4. *State of Popular Instruction.* ; to one five pounds, to another five
The annual reports of the Registrar, ι equal right to his share, but not a
test of the actual progress of elementar be enforced by an assertion that the
satisfactory to observe that it is not quite ι, of another man is to that other.
that " *one* in *three* of the young men, and any means, for a small all is not
England could not write their names in the A small all may be lost, and
in 1864, but *one* in *four* of the men, and one reat wisdom be risked for the
with marks.   be little or not at all worth
During the twenty-three years the proportion *didit.* But a large all can
of marks-men has fallen from 33 to 23; of mark cumulating, perhaps, from

Date.	Total Marriages in England.	Men who s with marks.	the product of a long life circumstances which will
1841	122,496	39,954	fast as they acquire it.
1864	147,914	41,998	s that the benefit and

The relative numbers of the ignorant to the ins, ibution, should be as
with the growth of the population, but the *absolut* xii. p. 611.
cated have undergone no diminution; and these fig universal. But, my
only, give no accurate idea of the neglected state of the members of a
country.   e in the government.
The Registrar General says (speaking of 1864):—" ay even be advanced
90 could write their names in Westmorland, 89 in L but from a share in
berland, 83 in the East Riding, 81 in the North Rid
Sussex, 80 in Cumberland, 80 in Devon. The pro,
descending deplorably from county to county until it t.
Hertford, and South Wales, 62 in Stafford, and 58 in .
cessive ignorance of the colliers of Staffordshire and rrupt practices at
incalculable evils, among others of explosions, and prob. Totnes, give us
The Registrar contrasts this state of things with t, wing illustration
round Aberdeen, where ninety-seven in every hundred ι hich the abolition
ninety-one in every hundred women, wrote their nam ghs, by the new
(p. xviii.) that " it is difficult to explain a difference so cree
in any other way than that, in the general struggle for the. rincipal briber
at the Reformation, the people had the good sense to endow. - as a witness
with small stipends, and not to give the whole revenue of t admitted; who
the clergy or to the nobility. Between the ministers and who was under
the schoolmasters in the presence of the people."   ne distribution
                                                        · uncil, but was

In England we are making the schoolmaster more and mor,
the minister, even for bread; and we lose our best teachers as ι
them by leaving them without a career. A good schoolmaste
without himself taking Holy Orders, because all Collegiate or ot
ments connected with public instruction of the slightest value abc
primary school, are allowed to be monopolised by the Clergy. T l's Report,
of a Government Inspector of Education (worth about £600 per an. Navy, and
for secular objects of instruction, at least, should have been especi ,__u,001,
as a prize for secular teachers, of experience and merit, is cy whole share
a new kind of Church living. This has arisen from "
grants being principally distributed through a Society '
patronage of the Bench of Bishops, called the *National St*
which may now be considered as, *de facto,* a branch of the
This Society stipulated as the condition of its co-operation, the
for Schools in connection with it should be persons appro
Archbishops of Canterbury and York. The present tot:

www.ingramcontent.com/pod-product-compliance
Lightning Source LLC
Chambersburg PA
CBHW021438090426
42739CB00009B/1529